Mikhail
GORBACHEV

ANDREW LANGLEY

Heinemann
LIBRARY

H www.heinemann.co.uk/library
Visit our website to find out more information about **Heinemann Library** books.

To order:
☎ Phone 44 (0) 1865 888066
▤ Send a fax to 44 (0) 1865 314091
▢ Visit the Heinemann Bookshop at www.heinemann.co.uk/library to browse our
catalogue and order online.

First published in Great Britain by
Heinemann Library, Halley Court, Jordan
Hill, Oxford OX2 8EJ, part of Harcourt
Education Ltd.

Heinemann is a registered trademark of
Harcourt Education Ltd.

Produced for Heinemann by Discovery Books
Ltd

Editorial: Patience Coster, Nicole Irving,
Andrew Solway and Jennifer Tubbs
Design: Ian Winton
Illustrator: Stefan Chabluk
Picture research: Rachel Tisdale
Production: Séverine Ribierre

Originated by Dot Gradations
Printed and bound in China by South China
Printing Company

ISBN 0 431 13882 6
07 06 05 04 03
10 9 8 7 6 5 4 3 2 1

**British Library Cataloguing in
Publication Data**
Langley, Andrew
 Mikhael Gorbachev. – (Leading lives)
 947'. 0854 '092

A full catalogue record for this book is
available from the British Library.

Acknowledgements
The publishers would like to thank the
following for permission to reproduce
photographs: Bettman/Corbis: pp. **22**, **30**, **33**,
36; Camera Press: pp. **6**, **9**, **11**; Corbis: pp. **15**
(Jim Zuckerman), **39**, **40**, **42**; Hulton Archive:
pp. **18**, **27**, **29**; Perfecto Romero/CSC: p. **44**;
Peter Newark's American Pictures: pp. **24**,
25; Popperfoto: pp. **4**, **21**, **23**, **26**, **32**, **48**, **51**;
Popperfoto/Reuters: p. **54**; Rex Features: pp.
5, **17**, **35**; South American Pictures: p. **52**
(Rolando Pujol).

Cover photograph of Mikhael Gorbachev
reproduced with permission of Popperfoto.

Every effort has been made to contact
copyright holders of any material
reproduced in this book. Any omissions will
be rectified in subsequent printings if notice
is given to the publishers.

Contents

Any words appearing in the text in bold, **like this**, are explained in the Glossary

The coup

Mikhail Gorbachev, president of the **Soviet Union**, was on holiday. He had travelled with his wife, daughter, son-in-law and grandchildren to his *dacha*, or country home, on the shore of the Black Sea. But he had little time to look at the view. On 18 August 1991 he was sitting at his desk, hard at work.

Late in the afternoon his chief guard entered. He told Gorbachev that a group of officials from Moscow had arrived to see him. Gorbachev was annoyed. He was not expecting any visitors. He reached for the telephone to find out what was happening. All five of the phone lines were dead. Now he was worried, and quickly told his family that he expected trouble.

Taking over power

At last the visitors were shown in. They had been sent, they said, by an Emergency Committee of the **Communist** Party which was now in charge of the Soviet Union. They told Gorbachev that the committee did not like his reform programme, which was bringing in great changes to the way the country was run. They feared that these changes were

▼ *Army tanks outside the **Kremlin** in Moscow immediately following the coup against Gorbachev in August 1991.*

leading to the break-up of the Soviet Union and the end of Communist Party power. He must agree to restore the Party's control – or resign.

Gorbachev was defiant and refused to agree to either of these demands even though he was in a very dangerous position. He was in fact a prisoner of his enemies. The next day a double ring of guards surrounded his *dacha*, the telephone and television were cut off and warships patrolled the shore. The only news of the outside world came through a little portable radio.

Defeat of the plotters

There was little that Gorbachev could do. His wife Raisa worried that the plotters might poison the family. A story that the president was ill had already been put out. She began to store food and, with her daughter, hid all the fruit in the house so that the grandchildren would not go hungry. That afternoon the family went down to the beach as usual. While the children swam, Gorbachev tried to think of a way out.

But the **coup** was already falling apart. Back in Moscow, the people had turned against the Emergency Committee. Huge crowds flocked to the White House, Russia's parliament building, to protect it from attack. The conspirators were arrested, and the power of the Communist Party was broken, after 70 years of absolute rule. The liberation of the Soviet Union, begun by Mikhail Gorbachev, was about to take another giant step forward.

▶ *Still looking slightly confused, Gorbachev holds a press conference on his return to Moscow after the coup failed.*

Child of the steppe

Mikhail Gorbachev was born on 2 March 1931 in the village of Privolnoye, in the Stavropol region of southern Russia. It was a remote spot, part of the vast rolling plain called the **steppe**, and it lay in the middle of some of the country's richest farmland. Gorbachev loved it.

FOR A MAP OF THE PLACES MENTIONED, SEE PAGE 9.

Gorbachev's parents were peasants and home was a simple three-roomed dwelling built of mud and straw. His father was a quiet but intelligent man who was in charge of the village's tractor station. His mother was a much stronger character, who had an important influence on young Mikhail's life.

▲ *Part of the vast rolling grasslands of the steppes in the Stavropol region where Gorbachev grew up.*

FOR DETAILS ON KEY PEOPLE OF GORBACHEV'S TIME, SEE PAGE 58.

Fear and famine

Stavropol, with its fertile soil and warm summers, was a perfect area for growing crops and raising livestock. Yet when Mikhail was a toddler many people there were starving. This was because Joseph Stalin, Russia's leader, wanted all peasants to join large, state-controlled **collective farms**. When a village such as Privolnoye refused to join, Stalin's men forcibly took away its food. During the winter of 1933-34, one third of Privolnoye's population starved to death. No wonder Gorbachev was a scrawny, underfed infant.

There was an even greater terror than famine. During the 1930s, Stalin's **secret police** arrested millions of people who were suspected of opposing his policies. Many were executed or sent to **labour camps**. In 1937 Gorbachev's own grandfather was taken away in the middle of the night. He was released a year later, but his tales of torture and imprisonment deeply shocked the young Mikhail.

Nazi invasion

In 1941, during World War Two, Gorbachev's father also left home, to fight with the Soviet army against the German **Nazis**, who had invaded Russia. The ten year-old Mikhail, as the only son, had to take on his father's role. Throughout the severe winter, he worked the family vegetable patch, gathered fuel for the stove and fed the cow. There was little time left for school.

German troops swept into Privolnoye in August 1942. They took all the villagers' food supplies, and threatened to execute all known **communists**. This included the Gorbachevs and so Mikhail went into hiding for a while in a nearby farmhouse. Early in 1943, Soviet troops liberated the region, but the Gorbachevs' troubles were far from over. Famine hit the village again, and Mikhail's mother was forced to take her husband's clothes to market, where she swapped them for food.

◀ *A Nazi trooper strides past a burning ammunition dump during the German invasion of Russia in 1941.*

By the end of 1944 the Germans had finally been driven out of Russia, though World War Two did not end until 1945. Slowly, things returned to normal. Mikhail went back to his primary school after a two-year gap, but after the horrors of wartime it seemed, he said, 'a waste of time'. His father came home from the army and resumed his job in the tractor workshop. The family grew, with the birth of a second son, Alexander. By this time, however, Mikhail was fifteen years old, and he never really became close to his much younger brother.

Work and secondary school

Gorbachev had worked on the collective farm during the war. By 1946 he was old enough to operate a combine harvester, cutting and gathering the wheat from the fields. It was gruelling work. In dry weather he laboured for up to twenty hours a day, with only three or four hours' sleep. The combine harvester had no cab so when it was cold he wrapped himself in straw to keep warm.

In 1948, Gorbachev began studying at the local secondary school. It was

◄ *Men and girls at work on a collective farm near the Black Sea in 1937. They are planting tobacco.*

Collective farms and children

From 1928, small farms were taken away from individual peasants and combined to form huge, state-controlled collective farms. One aim of this was to increase the production of food by using bigger fields and more machines.

Children such as Mikhail Gorbachev were expected to help with this often back-breaking labour. In 1942 a new law made it compulsory for all boys and girls aged twelve to sixteen to work for at least 50 days each year on the farm.

twenty kilometres (12.5 miles) away, so he had to walk there, renting a room nearby during the week and returning home to his family at the weekends.

Young communist

He studied hard and quickly became a star pupil, excelling in physics, chemistry, mathematics and history. At the same time he took his first steps in politics and joined the Communist Party's youth organization, called the **Komsomol**. Gorbachev was clearly eager to find success in the wider world far from Privolnoye. He could only do this as a Party member.

▼ *Gorbachev grew up in the Stavropol region of the **USSR** and spent his early working life there.*

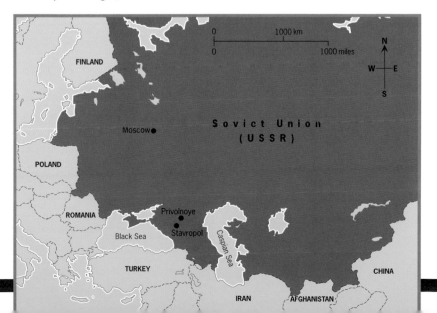

Moscow student

Mikhail Gorbachev left school with two awards. One was a silver medal for his school work. But he was always more proud of the other, the Order of the **Red Banner** of Labour, given for his heroic efforts on the combine harvester. This award was a vital help in his ambition to leave the **steppes** of Stavropol. Most of his friends were going to local colleges, but Gorbachev wanted something better – a place at Moscow State University. With his Red Banner award, he was soon accepted there.

Country boy in the capital

Gorbachev decided to study law, although at the time he had only a vague idea of what the law was all about! The main reason, he wrote later, was that 'the position of a judge or prosecutor impressed me'. Clearly, the young man was interested in powerful roles.

After the endless plains of Stavropol, Moscow seemed an exciting place to be. Gorbachev went to theatres and galleries

◀ *Moscow State University, where Gorbachev studied from 1950 to 1955. It was here that he met his future wife, Raisa.*

and visited Red Square, the **Kremlin** (the headquarters of the **Soviet Union**'s government) and other famous sites. But in the early months he felt ill at ease. He was obviously a peasant in the big city, proudly wearing his fur hat, his clumsy brown suit and his Red Banner medal. Some fellow students found him strange at first and mocked him, but they soon came to respect his fierce intelligence and energy.

Life at the university was not luxurious. Gorbachev lived in a huge hostel (accommodation for students) outside the city. In his first year he was squeezed into a dormitory with 21 others. He had to make do with food sent from home, and a shower in a public bathhouse twice a month.

Joining the Party

Gorbachev became a full member of the **Communist** Party at nineteen – the youngest possible age he could join. This act showed how ambitious he was. In Russia, nobody at that time could reach any position of authority without being a zealous and loyal Party member. Gorbachev wanted power, and he knew that, even as a communist, he would have to work very hard to get it. He would also have to please the right people and never ask awkward questions.

FOR MORE ABOUT STALIN, SEE PAGE 58.

He learned this the hard way. In 1952, he complained that one of his teachers was not lecturing at all, but simply reading aloud page after page from a book by Stalin. The reaction was one of shock and horror. No-one was expected to criticize their teachers – let alone the great Stalin! The scandal went as far as the Moscow committee of the Communist Party, but eventually Gorbachev was pardoned, thanks to his 'worker and peasant' background. He would be more careful in future.

Even so, he found it hard to stay quiet when he saw injustice being done. In early 1953 a wave of anti-Jewish feeling spread through Moscow. Gorbachev was enraged to discover that one of his colleagues, a Jew, had been insulted and even assaulted. On one occasion he leapt to his feet and fiercely defended his friend against the student mob – and that was the end of the persecution.

Raisa

Gorbachev had already found another focus for his passionate nature – a beautiful fellow student named Raisa Titorenko. Small and elegant, Raisa was studying philosophy (and she had gained a gold medal at school – one better than Gorbachev). He had first met her in 1951 and tried desperately to impress her, though he remembers, 'I think I made a terrible fool of myself.' But he persevered, and soon they were spending all their free time together. By 1953 they had decided to get married, even though they were still poor students.

Somehow, Gorbachev had to raise enough money for them to set up home. That summer, he returned to Privolnoye and worked hard as a mechanic at the tractor workshop. There was a bumper grain harvest that year, and Mikhail and his father sold their crop for nearly 1000 roubles (basic monetary unit of Russia) – a huge sum in those days. With his share, he was able to plan for the wedding.

Death of a dictator

In the midst of this, the whole Russian population suffered a massive shock. Joseph Stalin died in March 1953. He had been the nation's leader for 25 years and, even though millions had died during his rule, had come to be seen as an almost god-like figure by most Russians. Gorbachev was devastated by

▲ *The dead dictator Joseph Stalin lying-in-state in Moscow in 1953. Gorbachev was among the huge crowds that filed past the body.*

the death and joined thousands of others in filing past Stalin's open coffin.

Doubts began to surface in his mind as he stared at the corpse. 'I searched for traces of his greatness, but there was something disturbing in his appearance which created mixed feelings,' he wrote. Already, it was recognized that the Soviet state created by Stalin was unjust and doomed to fail. University friends described Gorbachev as a 'dissident' – someone who disagreed with the political system. It was a dangerous thing to be, but Gorbachev managed to keep his **liberal** views well hidden. On the surface, he was a devoted and energetic Communist Party member.

Back to Stavropol

Mikhail Gorbachev and Raisa were married in Moscow on 25 September 1953. They were still students, and at first the university authorities would not let them live together. Each night, they would go to their separate rooms. Gorbachev organized a protest by the student **Komsomol** against the ruling, and eventually he and his wife were given a room to share. 'I felt like a real family man,' he wrote happily.

▲ *Mikhail and Raisa Gorbachev early in their long married life.*

Shattered plans

But the happiness was short-lived. Gorbachev graduated from the university in 1955, and confidently assumed that he would be given a legal post in Moscow. When he reported to the state **Procurator's** office, however, he was told that there was no job for him. Law graduates were thought to be too young and innocent for the work involved.

This was shattering. His grand career seemed to have ended before it began. His only option was to return to his home district and find work there. He would also need to find somewhere for Raisa and himself to live. Leaving Raisa to stay with her parents for a month, Gorbachev packed up their few belongings in two suitcases and a wooden crate and boarded the train back to Stavropol, where he was soon taken on by the **District Prosecutor's** office.

Now he had to find somewhere to live. He rented a tiny shabby room, much of which was taken up by a stove and a long iron bed. There was no other furniture, so the crate came in useful as both a table and a bookcase. The lavatory was outside, and water had to be collected from a pump.

Change of direction

It was a bleak place for Raisa to come to. She was already pregnant, and had given up her postgraduate studies in Moscow to be with her husband. Worse still, Mikhail suddenly decided to accept an entirely new job – one that would take him away from the family home for several nights each week.

Gorbachev had hated the life of a lawyer. Even though Stalin was gone, his system of state control was still in place. This meant that most law cases were controlled by the politicians or even by the **KGB (secret police)** and had little to do with justice or fairness. To his great relief, Gorbachev's new post was with the local *Komsomol* in what was called the 'agitation and **propaganda** department'.

His job was to spread the ideas of **communism** among young people and encourage them to be model citizens. It meant a lot of travel around the district, even to the remotest villages – sometimes by train or truck but often on foot. No wonder he spent some of his first month's salary on a pair of sturdy boots.

Desolate villages

Gorbachev described what he saw when he and some other *Komsomol* workers visited a remote Stavropol village.

As far as the eye could see, scattered at random, [were] low, smoke-belching huts... Down there, in those miserable dwellings, people led some kind of life. But the streets (if you could call them streets) were deserted. As if the plague had ravaged the entire village... And I told myself that this was the reason why the young fled from this god-forsaken village. They fled from desolation and horror, from the terror of being buried alive.

People deserve a better life – that was always on my mind.

(From Mikhael Gorbachev's **memoirs**, 1995)

Political education

Gorbachev learned several important lessons from his time with the *Komsomol*. He saw for himself the desperate lives of those who lived in isolated areas. He noticed that many of the Communist Party bosses in the district were ignorant and greedy. Compared to other people the Party bosses looked very well-fed. 'When you look at one of the local leaders you see nothing outstanding apart from his belly,' he told Raisa. Perhaps most important of all, he learned to be a public figure, making speeches and answering questions.

▼ *Shabby houses, unpaved roads and mud everywhere – a typical village in Russia of the 1950s.*

◄ *Soviet leader Nikita Khrushchev waves to cheering crowds on a visit to Prague, the capital city of Czechoslovakia, in 1957.*

Gorbachev's political views were given another jolt in the spring of 1956. The new Soviet leader, Nikita Khrushchev, made a speech attacking the character and leadership of Joseph Stalin. This shocked the entire country, for nobody had previously dared to suggest that Stalin ever made mistakes. On his travels, Gorbachev was often asked to explain the meaning of Khrushchev's speech. Privately, he supported the leader's courageous step, which added to his own doubts about the oppressive way that the Soviet government worked.

FOR DETAILS ON KEY PEOPLE OF GORBACHEV'S TIME, SEE PAGE 58.

Starting a family

The Gorbachevs' only daughter, Irina, was born in January 1957. Their joy was clouded by the news that Raisa could never have another child. Life was difficult enough for her in any case. The lodgings were cold and cramped, baby food was unobtainable and the family now had to exist on one salary.

Slowly, things got better. When at last Raisa was able to return to work, she got a post at the local college, where she was paid more than her husband. Shortly after this, they were able to afford a two-roomed flat, though they had to share the lavatory and bathroom. Then, in 1958, Gorbachev was elected as second secretary of the Stavropol *Komsomol* committee. His march to the top had begun.

Looking for patrons

Gorbachev did not have long to wait for his next promotion. In March 1961 he became the **Komsomol's first secretary**, or leader, for the whole district. This brought him an official car for his travelling and a mountain of paperwork on his desk every day. This paperwork was mostly made up of directives from the **Central Committee**. It also took him onto a higher level in the local political world. Now he was mixing with more influential people.

Sideways and upwards

That October, Gorbachev rubbed shoulders with the most powerful figures in the land. For the first time he attended a **Party Congress** in Moscow as the Stavropol **delegate**. There he heard Khrushchev renew his attacks on Stalin and outline major reforms to the Soviet system. He admired Khrushchev's daring, but realized that the leader was gaining a lot of enemies who might eventually destroy him.

FOR A SUMMARY OF THE SOVIET SYSTEM OF GOVERNMENT, SEE PAGE 59.

Gorbachev knew that any politician, especially an ambitious peasant like himself, was bound to have enemies. What he needed were patrons, people in positions of power who could help and support him. Among the first of these was Fedor Kulakov, the Party boss for the region, who quickly realized that Gorbachev was an outstanding and hard-working young man. Promotion soon followed. In 1962 Gorbachev was transferred from the *Komsomol* to work directly for the **Communist** Party.

His new job was to supervise the work of the regional Communist Party in three agricultural districts. Now he had to work even harder. 'I spent days, and often nights, travelling around the district, visiting farms,' he wrote. Less than a year later he took another big step up the ladder when Kulakov

▶ *Fedor Kulakov, the wily Communist Party official whose influence helped to launch Gorbachev on his rise to the top.*

chose him to be head of the department which appointed Party officials in the region. This was a very responsible position and brought Gorbachev into almost daily contact with his boss.

The fall of Khrushchev

Kulakov was a valuable friend to have. He was fiercely ambitious, and was working his way up into the highest levels of the **Kremlin**. He was also cunning. When Khrushchev was in power, Kulakov agreed in public with everything he said, but in private he plotted against him with others who feared that the leader's reforms were going too far.

In October 1964 Khrushchev was finally overthrown and replaced by the more conservative Leonid Brezhnev. Kulakov immediately moved to Moscow where he became secretary for agriculture. Now Gorbachev had a patron near the very top. But he had also learned a valuable lesson from Khrushchev's fall: no leader could push through reforms if he had powerful enemies inside the Party.

FOR DETAILS ON KEY PEOPLE OF GORBACHEV'S TIME, SEE PAGE 58.

With Kulakov's support, Gorbachev moved steadily higher. In 1966 he became **first secretary** of Stavropol city's Party organization. This gave him more freedom to make his own decisions.

Learning from Raisa

Gorbachev was always very proud of his wife's achievements. When she taught philosophy classes at the Institute, he joined the course as a student. The pair would often hold heated debates about philosophical theories, but Raisa usually had the last word.

Raisa's views had a strong influence on her husband. To complete her Moscow State University doctorate (higher degree) in 1967, she had conducted research into the way **collective farms** were run. She found that farmers who were allowed to operate independently produced better crops than those who stayed under strict state control. Gorbachev learned a lot from her work.

Stagnation under Brezhnev

In August 1968 Gorbachev was summoned to Moscow, where he was told that he

◄ Smiles before tears: Brezhnev (centre) is greeted by the Czech leader Alexander Dubcek (far right) during an apparently friendly meeting in Bratislava. Soviet tanks arrived two weeks later to prevent Dubcek from carrying on with his liberal policies.

was now second-in-command of Party affairs in the whole of Stavropol. But he had hardly settled into this post before news came of the invasion of Czechoslovakia by **Warsaw Pact** armed forces.

Gorbachev was saddened by the brutal repression of the Czechs. At home, too, there was a renewed clampdown on anyone who questioned the Communist Party line or suggested reforms.

The suppression of the Czechs

Czechoslovakia had been governed by the Communist Party since 1948. This meant that it was really under Soviet rule, as part of the **Eastern bloc**. Alexander Dubcek became Party leader in 1968, and introduced many **liberal** reforms, such as freedom of the press and contact with non-communist countries. He promised 'socialism with a human face'.

Back in the **Kremlin**, there was anger and alarm. Brezhnev and other Soviet leaders believed that Dubcek's measures would weaken communist control in Czechoslovakia. They feared that calls for reform might spread to neighbouring communist countries that were also under Soviet control. So, in August 1968, over 200,000 Soviet troops, backed by small forces from other Warsaw Pact armies, invaded Czechoslovakia. Dubcek was arrested and imprisoned, and his place taken by hard-line officials. The country became an obedient communist state once again.

◀ A lone protestor tries vainly to stop Soviet tanks as they grind through the streets of Bratislava during the Soviet invasion of Czechoslovakia in 1968.

Party boss

In the spring of 1970 the Party leaders elected Gorbachev **first secretary** for the whole Stavropol territory. This was a position of real power at last. The first secretary was an important person, with the entire management system of the region under his control. No appointments could be made without his approval. Even more important, first secretaries made up the majority of the Party **Central Committee** for the country (which Gorbachev joined in 1971). Their votes had a big influence on government actions.

The outside world

Gorbachev's new post also brought him a precious privilege: he could make visits to **Western** Europe. Since 1966, he and Raisa had travelled to countries in **communist** Eastern Europe, including East Germany, Bulgaria and Czechoslovakia. But these were strictly run on Soviet lines, with state-controlled farming and industry, no freedom of speech and an unhappy atmosphere. Gorbachev was depressed to find **East Berlin** a 'cold and forbidding' place.

The Cold War

During World War Two the USA and the Soviet Union had fought on the same side. Almost immediately after the war ended (1945) a new conflict split the world. This time the USA and the Soviet Union, which had grown into the two most powerful nations on earth, were on opposing sides. What divided them was politics. The Soviet Union wanted to help spread communism to other countries, while the aim of the capitalist USA was to prevent this. The two sides never confronted each other in battle and so the war was never a 'hot' one. The hostility felt between the two powers was described by a US politician in 1947 as a 'cold' war.

Now he could travel through the '**Iron Curtain**' to the **capitalist** West – something few Russians were allowed to do. In 1972 he and Raisa visited Belgium and the Netherlands. This was followed during the 1970s by trips to Italy, France and West Germany.

Gorbachev was astounded by what he saw. The Soviet news media were so tightly controlled that little information about the West ever reached ordinary people in the **Soviet Union**. As a result many Russians were ignorant and mistrustful of the West. Suddenly, he discovered that people in Western Europe could be open and honest in their opinions about things, including their governments. Even more shocking was the fact that their wealth and living conditions were much higher than those of people at home. How could a capitalist society work so much better than a **socialist** one?

Living standards

The question haunted me: why was the standard of living in our country lower than in other developed countries? It seemed that our aged leaders were not especially worried about our lower living standards, our unsatisfactory way of life, and our falling behind in the field of advanced technologies.

(From Mikhael Gorbachev's **memoirs**, 1995)

New patrons

By the mid-1970s, Gorbachev had found two new and powerful allies. One was Mikhail Suslov, a cunning and sinister politician who had worked for both Stalin and Khrushchev. The other was Yuri Andropov, head of the Soviet Union's dreaded **secret police**, the **KGB**. Andropov was an intelligent and honest man who was secretly appalled at the corrupt and stifling atmosphere of Brezhnev's leadership. He soon realized that Gorbachev was someone he could trust, and one who looked to a better future.

FOR DETAILS ON KEY PEOPLE OF GORBACHEV'S TIME, SEE PAGE 58.

Agricultural change

Gorbachev had something to prove. He was in a position of real authority, and now he had to show that he could take big decisions and put major plans into effect. Stavropol was an ideal place to make an impact. This key farming region was desperately in need of improvements to make its harvests bigger and its methods more efficient.

Gorbachev began by tackling the crop failures caused by drought. Back in Stalin's time, the first steps had been taken to build a canal which would bring precious water to the dry, windswept area. But the work had crawled along and it was still not completed. The **first secretary** flung all his enormous energy into the project. He wrote action plans, pestered ministers and even made a direct approach to Brezhnev himself. The result was spectacular and by 1978 the Stavropol Canal was finished.

There were other big problems to solve. How much grain should be grown? Was there enough food for the cattle and pigs to eat through the winter? How could the output of meat be increased quickly? Gorbachev found solutions to all these questions, often by challenging the decisions of the central government.

Even so, he could not win every battle. Thanks partly to Raisa's research into **collective farming**, Gorbachev had encouraged independent farmers. He allowed small groups to cultivate plots of land in whatever way they wanted. This was a spectacular success, and harvests on these plots improved by 600 per cent. But in 1977 Kulakov, the agriculture secretary in Moscow, decreed that a new system had to be put in place. Huge gangs of labourers now did the harvest work, marching across the country like an army. Gorbachev was forced to abandon his experiment.

Farewell to the steppe

Gorbachev's achievements at Stavropol marked him out as an up-and-coming politician. His first patron, Kulakov, died in 1978, but he still had the powerful support of Suslov and Andropov. He also grew closer to the prime minister, Aleksei Kosygin, and the pair would go for long walks together in the hills near the Black Sea.

The death of Kulakov left a vacancy in the **Politburo** – the very highest circle of communist power, where crucial decisions were made. Who would fill it? To his surprise, Gorbachev was appointed as the new secretary for agriculture, thanks to the influence of Andropov and the grudging approval of Brezhnev. With one bound he was inside the **Kremlin**.

He and Raisa were sad to leave the peace and natural beauty of Stavropol, where they had lived so long and raised their only daughter (Irina had been married that spring). Now the whole Gorbachev family had to make themselves a new home in faraway Moscow.

▼ *The ornate exterior of the Grand Kremlin Palace in Moscow, the main centre of Soviet government. Gorbachev returned to Moscow in 1978. His new job at the Kremlin was as secretary for agriculture.*

In the Politburo

Moscow seemed to have become a strange and unfriendly place since he had been a student there, and it took them some weeks to find a place to live. 'To begin with', wrote Gorbachev, 'we felt lonely.' He plunged straight into work, though many people in the **Central Committee** looked on him as just a country bumpkin from the provinces. Eventually, the family (including Irina and her husband Anatoly) moved into a comfortable apartment, and were given a *dacha* on the river near the city.

A shrinking economy

Gorbachev soon made an impact in the highest levels of government. He worked in his office for up to fifteen hours a day. He buzzed about the **Kremlin**, asking questions, singing and cracking jokes, but always anxious to learn and understand what was going on. His energy and enthusiasm led one dazed colleague to exclaim, 'He's an insatiable hurricane of a person.'

But the more he learned, the more uneasy he grew. The truth was that the **Soviet Union's** economy was falling apart. State-run factories and farms were so inefficiently organized that hundreds of thousands of labourers never bothered to go to work. Most products, such as tractors and cars, were of poor quality. The rural economy was in tatters as massive loans to the **collective farm** system could not be repaid. Bad farming practices had also contributed to the decline in the quality of crop-growing land. Worst of all, one quarter of the government's budget (money available to spend) was wasted on producing weapons, trying to keep up with the USA in the 'arms race'. Brezhnev and the other ageing leaders closed their eyes to the growing difficulties.

Mounting crisis

Gorbachev had his own problems. Now that he was in charge of the whole country's agriculture, he saw that there was going to be a shortage of food. The 1979 harvest was poor, and so he proposed **liberal** changes to the collective farming system to encourage better yields. He also asked that vital extra grain should be purchased from the USA.

The arms race

Since the 1960s, the military competition between the USA and the **USSR** had gathered speed. Massive sums of money were spent building all kinds of arms – especially **nuclear weapons** – in a race to gain superiority. By 1980, the two sides had 40,000 nuclear warheads between them. This gigantic store of weapons was enough to destroy life on earth several times over.

In the late 1970s the two sides tried to agree on ways of avoiding this terrible threat. They had signed a **Strategic Arms** Limitation Treaty in 1979 to restrict the number of nuclear weapons produced. A year later USA withdrew from this in protest at the Soviet invasion of Afghanistan.

The invasion of Afghanistan

On Christmas Day 1979, Soviet tanks and troops invaded Afghanistan in an attempt to strengthen the **socialist** government there. The conflict was a complete catastrophe. The huge Soviet army, with all its modern weapons, was unable to defeat the poorly-armed **Islamic resistance fighters**. Worse still, the invasion outraged the rest of the world. In protest, the USA broke off **trade agreements** and refused to sell any of its grain to the Soviet Union.

▲ *The beginning of a nightmare: Soviet tanks arrive in Afghanistan in 1979 at the start of the ill-fated invasion.*

Suddenly, agriculture became a hot topic. Gorbachev now had the chance to draw up bold plans for improving the country's farming and avoiding the need to buy supplies from abroad. He worked hard, studying research, consulting experts and battling to get his ideas accepted. In the end his Food Programme, introduced in 1982, was a costly failure – largely because corrupt officials used it for their own ends.

The Politburo's old men

The Afghan War was yet another disaster for the Soviet leaders. By this time government had reached a standstill, with no-one prepared to make tough decisions. The meetings of the **Politburo** (the average age of its members was over 70) became almost a joke. Brezhnev was ill, drugged and sometimes drunk, and few on the Committee could hear what he said. Andropov and other senior members were only interested in taking his place as soon as he died.

Gorbachev also discovered that work got in the way of his social life. He had little time for his family or for rest. Meeting his colleagues outside the office, or visiting their homes, was not encouraged. Politburo members were afraid that Brezhnev might get to hear about such meetings and conclude that people were plotting against him in private.

Raisa found it difficult to adjust to the limited kind of life among the 'Kremlin wives'. She thought them dull and arrogant, and made all her friends outside the tight government circle. She went back to college, and began to study English. With Mikhail, she enjoyed exploring the historic parts of the city of Moscow, and attending plays, operas and concerts – something few other Politburo couples would have done.

Death of Brezhnev

The old centre of Soviet power began to break up when Suslov died in January 1982. Andropov seized his place as deputy leader – he made sure of it by grabbing his chair at a Politburo session! By now Brezhnev, who was very ill, could not hold a pen or speak in public. Although his state of health was kept a secret from the Soviet people, he was surrounded by an emergency medical team. He died in November. Could this be the end of the long period of **stagnation**?

Life under Andropov

The new **general secretary** of the Soviet Union was one of Gorbachev's biggest political friends – Yuri Andropov. This meant promotion and much more responsibility. Gorbachev took over Andropov's position as second-in-command of the Party, and was placed in charge of the country's economy. Among the perks of his new job was a visit to Canada, where he impressed everyone with his intelligence and sense of humour.

FOR DETAILS ON KEY PEOPLE OF GORBACHEV'S TIME, SEE PAGE 58.

Andropov at last had the chance to introduce reforms in the Soviet Union and to forge a warmer relationship with the USA. He began energetically, with campaigns against corrupt officials, poor work performance and excessive drinking. He opened talks with the US president, Ronald Reagan, on reducing the numbers of nuclear missiles in Europe.

But these projects never succeeded. Andropov, like Brezhnev, was old and sick, and rumours began to spread that he would not last long. When he died in February 1984, members of the **Politburo** were still afraid to look to the future. Gorbachev was the obvious choice as new leader, but most thought that at aged 53 he was too young! So they elected Konstantin Chernenko instead, who was 73 years old and dying from asthma and other diseases.

◀ *Gorbachev (front row second right) stands with other Soviet leaders to pay his last respects to Yuri Andropov in 1984.*

◀ *The Gorbachevs on their first visit to Britain in 1984. Mikhail is greeted by Prime Minister Margaret Thatcher and Raisa by Denis Thatcher.*

For the third time, the Soviet people were led by someone who was elderly, feeble and out of touch.

Last of the old men

Now Gorbachev had to be patient, as he was clearly next in line for the leadership. Fortunately he had plenty to do, for with Chernenko too ill to travel he became the country's representative. In June 1984, Gorbachev led the Party delegation to Italy to attend the funeral of the Italian communist leader Enrico Berlinguer.

A few months later he and Raisa made their first visit to Great Britain, where they met the forceful British prime minister, Margaret Thatcher. The trip was a huge success. The British public were amazed to find that Raisa was glamorous and lively – nothing like other Soviet wives they had seen. And Mrs Thatcher quickly warmed to Mikhail's charm and energy. 'I like Mr Gorbachev,' she said. 'We can do business together.'

Some of the older **Kremlin** leaders were jealous of Gorbachev's popularity at home and abroad. But they were too late to stop his rise to power, for he had great support from regional officials. As Chernenko became more ill, Gorbachev started taking the chair at weekly Politburo meetings. When the old general secretary died in March 1985, the members had no choice but to propose that Mikhail Gorbachev should take his place.

Soviet leader

On 10 March 1985 the **Central Committee** of the Soviet **Communist** Party elected Mikhail Gorbachev as their new **general secretary**. He responded with a speech setting out his aims. He said that the **Soviet Union** had to move forward by developing its science and technology, and by improving its society in a more just and **democratic** way. The Party and the state would operate with greater *glasnost* (openness). He declared that he wanted to stop the arms race with the **West** and to reduce the number of **nuclear weapons**.

FOR A SUMMARY OF THE SOVIET SYSTEM OF GOVERNMENT, SEE PAGE 59.

Building a power base

Many general secretaries had spoken like this in the past. Few Russians expected that this stocky peasant from Stavropol would keep his promises any better than previous leaders. But Gorbachev was not only determined to make major changes to the Soviet system, he was also cunning enough to push the

▼ *Gorbachev's only child Irina (left) with her daughter Kseniya and husband Anatoly at a Red Square military parade in 1985.*

changes through. He knew that all new measures had to be approved by the **Politburo** and he could not work without its support.

So his first task was to shuffle the members of the Politburo so that most of them were on his side. He got rid of the old guard from the Brezhnev era. This included the long-time foreign minister Andrei Gromyko (known in the West as 'Grim Grom' because of his negative attitude), who was given the less important job of Soviet president. Then Gorbachev gave powerful posts to younger, more **liberal** men.

Outside the Politburo he was just as ruthless. Half of the department heads were sacked, as were 39 out of 101 Soviet ministers. Throughout the Soviet Union about 20 per cent of all officials were replaced with new men. (Women were not given any of the top political jobs.) Reform was in the air as Gorbachev stamped his authority on the government from the beginning.

Meeting the people

Next, he did something even more extraordinary. He started making regular visits to factories and towns, mingling with people and talking to them. Raisa often went with him. Gorbachev wanted to hear what ordinary Russians had to say, and he scolded local officials who tried to silence them when he was present. No Soviet leader had ever acted so openly and freely before.

As Soviet leader Gorbachev had little free time to pursue other interests. When time was available he liked to visit the theatre and art galleries with Raisa. Finding some time to enjoy the peace of the countryside was also important to him.

◀ *Breaking the ice: US President Ronald Reagan and Gorbachev share a joke during their first summit meeting in 1985.*

Star Wars and summits

The Soviet economy was by that time in an even worse mess. Gorbachev knew that spending on defence was one of the major causes of this. Every year, huge sums were swallowed up to build weapons and maintain the armed forces. Even so, the Soviet Union was falling behind the USA, which had suddenly increased its build-up of arms. Most worrying of all was the '**Star Wars**' project – a US scheme to install a defence system out in space which would destroy enemy missiles with laser beams.

Gorbachev had to start new talks on halting the arms race. He arranged a '**summit**' meeting with US President Ronald Reagan in Geneva, Switzerland, for November 1985. For the first time in many years the heads of the **capitalist** and communist worlds talked together in a warm and constructive way. At the end of three days they signed a joint declaration. 'Nuclear war cannot be won and must never be fought,' they said, and they promised to improve relations between the two countries.

Retreat from Afghanistan

The two men held their second summit meeting a year later in Reykjavik, Iceland – halfway between the USA and the **USSR**. Once again they edged closer to agreement on reducing arms and even getting rid of nuclear weapons. But no definite treaty was signed and the **superpowers** remained suspicious of each other.

The US knew that the Soviet Union was still in a terrible mess, both at home and abroad, and could not be relied on.

Chernobyl

The Soviet authorities had always told everyone that the nuclear power plant at Chernobyl, in Ukraine, was perfectly safe. Then on 26 April 1986 one of the reactors blew up killing 31 people at once and injuring over 500 others.

The blast spread a cloud of dangerous **radioactive dust** over large parts of Europe, and crops grown in these areas had higher than normal levels of radiation. Fortunately this effect wore off quite quickly. Around Chernobyl, however, radiation levels had long term consequences. In the next five years thousands of people in the Chernobyl area died of **leukaemia** and other illnesses.

Their fears increased in mid-1986 after news of a massive explosion at a **nuclear power plant** at Chernobyl. If a tragic accident like that could happen, how could the Soviets be trusted to control their nuclear weapons?

Gorbachev was certainly sincere in wanting an end to the **Cold War** – and to other wars. The most obvious of these was the war in Afghanistan, which was still dragging on. Despite the many Russian casualties there was still no success. Gorbachev called it 'a running sore'. In November 1986 he withdrew 6000 Soviet troops from Afghanistan. This still left over 90,000, but it was the start of a long drawn-out retreat from disaster.

▲ *The wreckage of the fourth block of the Chernobyl nuclear power plant.*

Glasnost and perestroika

By early 1987, Gorbachev had good reason to be hopeful. Abroad, he found a fresh ally in his search for peace and stability. The British prime minister, Margaret Thatcher, visited Moscow. Although strongly anti-**communist**, she liked Gorbachev's energetic and aggressive way of conducting affairs, which was very like her own. Once again, the two enjoyed a frank and warm discussion, sometimes shouting, sometimes laughing. From now on, Thatcher worked hard to improve the relationship between Gorbachev and Reagan, helping to smooth out differences and misunderstandings between them.

Rebuilding the USSR

At home, Gorbachev believed that two new policies would turn the **Soviet Union** away from the decay, corruption and nightmares of its past – *glasnost* and *perestroika*. *Glasnost* means 'openness', and for the first time in Soviet history the

▼ *Gorbachev made many trips around the country to meet the Russian people. Here he talks to factory workers near Moscow in 1987.*

Russian people were encouraged to talk honestly about their government and to make criticisms. Foreign radio stations, such as the BBC and Voice of America, were officially allowed to broadcast. Books once banned as anti-communist were published at last. By mid-1987, over 300 **political prisoners** had been set free.

Perestroika means 'rebuilding'. Gorbachev was determined to transform the country's economy and industry into something that worked on modern, open lines. This included what was called 'the human factor' – taking more notice of what ordinary workers wanted, and how they were treated. Much more money was to be invested in factories and the creation of new industries.

The backlash

But this more **liberal** rule brought its own problems. Russians now felt bold enough to criticize Gorbachev himself. Many stalwart communists hated the way that much of the Party's power had been taken away. Also ordinary people found that the rebuilding of the economy did not necessarily mean that working and living conditions improved. Gorbachev was angry with the moaners who wanted, he said, 'to improve things without changing anything'.

One of his fiercest critics was Boris Yeltsin, a rough, tough member of the **Politburo**. In October 1987 he caused a sensation by claiming that *perestroika* was moving too slowly, that Gorbachev's promises were empty and that fellow members were bullies. Gorbachev was furious. A few days later he forced Yeltsin to resign, saying, 'I will never allow you back into big-time politics.' Little did he know that he had made a powerful enemy.

FOR DETAILS ON KEY PEOPLE OF GORBACHEV'S TIME, SEE PAGE 58.

▲ *Still smiling, Gorbachev and Reagan sign the historic arms agreement treaty in December 1987 which banned medium range nuclear missiles.*

Summit success

In December, Gorbachev went to the USA to meet President Reagan for a third **summit** conference in the capital city of Washington DC. This was a crucial meeting, a last chance to agree on ways to end the long **Cold War**. Once again, the pair got on well and a treaty was drawn up which swept away hundreds of nuclear missiles from Europe. The signing of the treaty was a significant worldwide event, which was shown live on television in both the USA and the Soviet Union.

The US public loved the Gorbachevs. A wave of 'Gorbymania' spread through Washington as the couple toured the streets, talking and shaking hands. *Time* magazine voted Mikhail its 'Man of the Year' for his part in promoting world peace. At a farewell dinner, he gave an emotional speech, saying 'What we have achieved is … a revival of hope.'

Six months later, Reagan and Gorbachev built on their achievements at a fourth summit. This time it was held in Moscow. They made some progress in agreeing to get rid of more **nuclear weapons**, but the biggest success was in opening up the Soviet Union to the outside world. Reagan became the first US president to talk to ordinary Russian citizens. He also made a speech to Moscow students and met critics of the government. This would never have been allowed to happen before Gorbachev became leader.

A new kind of government

Gorbachev had yet more surprises up his sleeve. At the Party Conference in June 1988, he proposed that the country should be run in the future by a single president and a **Congress of People's Deputies**. These would be chosen by the people in free elections. Until this point, the Communist Party had been the only political party allowed in the Soviet Union. Communists therefore had held all the most important positions of power – and the Party strictly controlled all elections. Now there could be open competition. It spelled the end of **one-party** rule.

The modernizing programme was pushed further ahead at a Party meeting in September. Several old men retired to make way for younger ones. Among the veterans was Andrei Gromyko, who had held the title of president, though he had no real power. Who would take his place? The answer was Gorbachev, who was quickly elected to the post. He was now both the Communist Party's **general secretary** and the Soviet Union's head of state.

The Iron Curtain disappears

On 7 December 1988, Gorbachev rose to make one of the most important speeches of his life. He was in the **United Nations** building in New York, talking to representatives from more than 150 countries.

Soviet leaders before him would have spoken of the class struggle, of great **communist** achievements and of US aggression. Gorbachev was entirely different. He declared an end to the **Cold War**, an end to his country's isolation from the **Western** world and the beginning of people's freedom to choose for themselves. He topped this by announcing that the size of the Soviet army was to be cut by half a million men.

His audience was stunned – and then they gave him a standing ovation. He became a hero throughout the USA. Crowds chanted 'Gorby! Gorby!' wherever he appeared.

▼ *Gorbachev makes his stirring speech to the United Nations General Assembly in 1988, promising a major cut in Soviet armed forces.*

The gathering storm

Back home, it was a different matter. Traditional communists were horrified at what Gorbachev's policy of free choice would mean to the countries of the **Eastern bloc**. These neighbouring countries had been under Soviet control for 40 years. Now they could choose to go their own way. Worse still, the **Soviet Union** itself, which was made up of fifteen separate **republics**, was in danger of splitting up.

Their fears were soon confirmed. In January 1989, Estonia, one of the Soviet republics, made the first attempt at acting for itself. A new law was passed which required all residents to be able to speak the Estonian language. Other republics quickly adopted the same laws for their own languages. It was a small step on the road to independence from Moscow, but it was a significant one.

FOR A MAP OF THE PLACES MENTIONED, SEE PAGE 52.

Soviet troops had always been there to back up unpopular communist governments in Eastern Europe. Now they were being brought home. People felt free to air their views. In Hungary, the parliament passed **liberal** new laws. Hungarian soldiers began cutting down the wire fences which lined their border with Austria. Protests and demonstrations broke out in Czechoslovakia as well as in the Soviet republics of Azerbaijan and Georgia.

The Eastern bloc

'An **iron curtain** has descended across the continent' said British Prime Minister Winston Churchill in 1946. He meant that Europe was split between the communist East and the **capitalist West**. The western countries were largely free and independent. Those in the East were tightly controlled by the Soviet Union, which organized communist governments in each one. The division of the continent was symbolized by the Berlin Wall, built across the middle of the city of Berlin by the communists in 1961 to prevent people fleeing to the West.

Rejecting communism

As Gorbachev had promised, in March 1989 the Soviet people were able to vote in the first free poll they had ever known. They were electing their first **democratic** parliament, for the **USSR Congress of People's Deputies**. The result of the election was a bitter blow for the Communist Party. Even though the majority of members won their seats, there was a large minority (20 per cent) who lost. Communists had never before believed that they could fail in an election.

Many powerful members of the Communist Party were defeated, while outsiders and independent candidates triumphed. One of those who shot back to power was Boris Yeltsin. A staggering 5 million people voted him in as mayor of Moscow. As expected, Gorbachev was elected as president by the ruling Congress committee, but Yeltsin's return must have been a worrying sign. It showed that people wanted to see faster change and so were prepared to support more radical politicians.

The fall of the Berlin Wall

Outside Russia things were happening with bewildering speed. Communist Eastern Europe, which had once seemed as solid as a rock, was suddenly falling to pieces as Soviet control over the region disappeared. In June 1989, the people of Poland threw the Communist Party from power in a free election. The Hungarian government opened its borders to allow people to flee through the country from East Germany to the West.

Gorbachev made it clear that he would not interfere with this process. In October, he visited **East Berlin**, the capital city divided by a concrete wall, where he was met by hordes of demonstrators shouting '*Perestroika*! Gorbachev! Help us!' and 'We need freedom!' The demonstrators had been demanding that East Germany be democratized and that political corruption be investigated.

East Berlin was now the focus of the freedom movement. The protests grew bigger and louder. A few weeks later, on 9 November, the government was forced to open its borders to the West. At least half a million people gathered on either side of the hated wall and began to attack the concrete with chisels and crowbars. All over the world, TV viewers watched in amazement as this symbol of the Cold War was destroyed.

▼ *Ecstatic crowds pour through a breach in the Berlin Wall in November 1989. This event marked the beginning of the end of Soviet control in Eastern Europe.*

FOR A MAP OF THE PLACES MENTIONED, SEE PAGE 52.

The amazing transformation galloped on. In Bulgaria, a reform group took over the national **Politburo**. In Czechoslovakia, the Communist Party was swept from office and replaced by reformers, among the leaders was Alexander Dubcek, who had led the liberal movement back in 1968. Romania, which had suffered years of economic **stagnation** and repressive government, followed their example in December when a violent revolutionary **coup** brought down the hated communist **dictator** Nikolai Ceaucescu. He was executed by firing squad. By the New Year of 1990, the communist empire in Eastern Europe was gone.

Trouble on the doorstep

The year 1989 had been a triumphant one for Gorbachev. With his enormous energy and idealism he had driven through reforms which had changed the face of Europe. He had helped to bring an end to the Cold War. He had given his countrymen and women free elections, and encouraged liberal governments in the Eastern bloc. On trips abroad he was treated as a hero. At the end of the year he had met the Pope in Rome, and held an important **summit** meeting with the new US president, George Bush.

But Gorbachev had made one major error. He believed that he could regulate the speed and spread of change, but it was soon like a runaway train. This was especially clear back home in the Soviet Union. For a start, the economy was in ruins. His policy of perestroika may have got rid of the stifling state control of industry, but it also exposed the fact that the country was running at a massive loss. Prices were rising, standards of living were falling and many people found themselves out of work.

Gorbachev's policy of *glasnost* may have given people the freedom to criticize government, but it also meant that he faced growing opposition from two sides. The old-fashioned Party members thought that he was betraying the ideals of the 1917 **Russian Revolution** and abandoning the strict communist code. Ordinary workers, on the other hand, wanted much more freedom and an end to the Party's hold on power. They began to go on **strike** for higher wages and for a bigger say in how their companies were managed.

Rebellious republics

Then there was the future of the Soviet Union itself. Gorbachev had encouraged the **satellite countries** of Eastern Europe to become independent of Moscow, so it was not surprising that the individual Soviet republics demanded liberty as well. This, for Gorbachev, was going too far. If the fifteen republics were released to govern themselves, the Soviet Union would be destroyed. It could not be allowed to happen.

However, the republics were utterly determined to break away, even if this brought bloodshed. As early as April 1989, a massive demonstration in Tbilisi, the capital city of Georgia, had been broken up by Soviet troops using truncheons (a short thick stick used as a weapon by police) and poison gas. Nineteen Georgians had died. In January 1990 Gorbachev travelled to Lithuania to try to persuade the people that they should stay inside the Union. But the Lithuanians ignored his speeches, and in March they declared their independence and elected their own president. Gorbachev's worst nightmare was coming true.

End of an empire

FOR A MAP OF THE PLACES MENTIONED, SEE PAGE 52.

The situation grew steadily worse throughout 1990. After Lithuania's defiance, more **republics** announced that they were breaking away from the **Soviet Union** – Estonia in March, Latvia in May and Ukraine in July. They were later followed by Belarus, Turkmenistan, Tajikistan and others. Gorbachev tried harsh methods to keep control. He cut off oil supplies to Lithuania, and sent troops to impose order in the capital city, Vilnius, but nothing could stop the rush towards independence.

▲ *On the streets of Vilnius, a woman gives out soup to demonstrators protesting at the Soviet crackdown in Lithuania.*

The Party's over

Gorbachev was now in an impossible position. One side thought he was changing things too fast, the other thought he was not changing them fast enough. This could be seen most clearly in the argument about the **Communist** Party. At a **Central Committee** meeting in February, Gorbachev proposed that there should no longer be just one political party in the Soviet Union. The Communist Party must give up its leading role. This caused a stormy debate, but the proposals were accepted.

In March the **Congress of People's Deputies** elected Gorbachev as president of the Soviet Union, and gave him more wide-ranging powers to govern. He was still a loyal member of the Communist Party and it seemed that he was in a very strong position. But, in fact, he was getting left behind by the speed of change.

A parallel president

Gorbachev found that his popularity was plummeting. He had given people more freedom, but he could not provide jobs, opportunities or hope for the future. There were still pitiful shortages in the shops, and even bread was hard to find. At the annual May Day Parade (to honour working people) in Moscow, he was greeted with jeers and roars of 'Resign!' by angry members of the crowd.

The next blow fell a few weeks later, when the Congress of People's Deputies in Russia elected a new chairman. They rejected the official Communist candidate. Instead, they chose a man who had resigned from the Communist Party and the **Politburo**, defied Gorbachev and won enormous support – Boris Yeltsin.

'We haven't just seized an office,' said Yeltsin. 'We have seized the whole of Russia!' He was right. Gorbachev might be the leader of the Soviet Union as a whole, but Yeltsin was leader of by far the biggest and most important part of it. Russia controlled much of the Soviet Union's trade and industry, and was the centre of finance and government. Within a fortnight, Yeltsin announced that Russia was a **sovereign state** – which meant that it too had declared its independence from the Soviet Union.

The crisis grows

Once again, Gorbachev found he had more friends and supporters abroad than at home. It was a rollercoaster ride. In October 1990 he was given the **Nobel Prize** for peace, one of the most important of all international awards. In November, a protestor fired shots at him during a parade in Moscow (luckily he was not hurt). Two weeks later, he signed a vital new treaty to limit troop numbers in Europe. In December foreign minister Eduard Shevardnadze, once one of Gorbachev's closest allies, resigned from his post, warning of the danger of **dictatorship** in the Soviet Union.

The year 1991 began grimly in the Baltic republics, which were still making angry demands for independence.

◄ *Gorbachev receiving the Nobel Peace Prize in October 1990. While many in the **Western** world welcomed his reforms, others within the Communist Party felt that Gorbachev's policies were going too far, and might result in the break up of the USSR.*

Bloodstained hands

During the 1991 meeting of the Congress of People's Deputies, Ales Adamovich, a Russian filmmaker, made a speech warning Gorbachev of the tragedy that would follow should he be tempted to use force in order to halt the break up of the Soviet Union.

The president will soon be surrounded by colonels and generals. Gorbachev is the only leader in Soviet history who has not stained his hands with blood, and we would like to remember him for that. But a moment will come when they will instigate a bloodbath, and later they will wipe their bloodstained hands against your suit, and you will be to blame for everything.

◄ *Moldovans rejoice in 1991 after their parliament declared its independence from Soviet control.*

Gorbachev ordered paratroops to seize public buildings in Vilnius; thirteen Lithuanians were killed. There was more bloodshed in Riga, the Latvian capital, where five protestors died in clashes with Soviet soldiers. Too late, Gorbachev realized he was making a terrible mistake and withdrew the troops – but he was already being seen by many as a hard-line bully. Georgia declared its break away from the Soviet Union in April.

Losing control

Meanwhile Boris Yeltsin was building up massive support as Russia's leader. He signed an agreement with the Baltic states, promising to give military help when needed against outside attacks. In June he won the country's first **democratic** poll to elect an official president of Russia. Now there really were two rival bosses ruling much the same territory; only Yeltsin was in a much stronger position than Gorbachev.

The Soviet leader made desperate efforts to avoid disaster and regain his reputation. He completed a new treaty with the USA, which cut the number of nuclear missiles on both sides. He tried, in vain, to organize a vast money loan from the USA to help the Soviet economy. Finally, he drew up a new plan for the Union, which he called the Nine Plus One Agreement. This would abolish the old **USSR** and replace it with a looser Union of Sovereign States, made up of nine republics plus Russia. In need of a break he flew off with his family for a holiday in their *dacha* by the Black Sea.

Time had run out for Mikhail Gorbachev. The rise of the anti-**communist** Yeltsin, the coming shake-up of the **Soviet Union**, the disappearance of the Soviet empire in Europe, the end of Communist Party supremacy, the unrest in the streets of Moscow – all of these events horrified the old guard of the **Kremlin**. Now they were taking action. While the Gorbachevs were safely out of the way, a group of senior Communist Party officials hatched their plot to seize power. Among the members of this 'Emergency Committee' were the Soviet vice-president, the head of the **KGB**, the prime minister and the defence minister.

The collapse of the coup

'I would not say that my holiday that year was a real rest,' wrote Gorbachev later. He was put under house arrest by the Emergency Committee. Raisa was, as always, a tower of strength. After four days of fear and uncertainty, the danger suddenly disappeared as the plot collapsed and the Gorbachevs were free to go back to Moscow.

Why did the **coup** fail? To begin with the members of the 'Emergency Committee' had no real plan. Even when they appeared on TV to announce the takeover, they looked weak and confused. The people of Russia simply did not take them seriously as leaders.

Then there was the swaggering figure of Boris Yeltsin. At this moment of crisis for the whole of Russia, he stood firmly on the side of Gorbachev's **liberal** reforms. When the Russian parliament building was under threat from the plotters, he climbed on top of a tank and rallied support against them. His bravery and defiant words made him an instant hero for ordinary people.

▲ *Boris Yeltsin becomes the hero of the Soviet people by refusing to surrender the parliament building to the coup leaders. His defiance rallied public support against the coup.*

A different country

Gorbachev, on the other hand, never recovered his authority. When he arrived at Moscow airport on 22 August, he announced that he was 'a different person returning to a different country', but he had failed to realize how much the Soviet Union had changed in a few days. Thousands of Moscow citizens demonstrated outside the headquarters of the hated KGB, then marched on the **Central Committee** building.

In spite of all his astonishing achievements, Gorbachev was now out of touch with what people wanted. He could not accept that the communist era was over – even when it was shown that the coup leaders had all been senior communists. His appearance in the Russian parliament was humiliating. Members jeered him, and Yeltsin forced him to read out the names of the plotters. The following day he resigned as leader of the Soviet Communist Party.

Bit by bit, Gorbachev's world was crumbling around him. He closed down the Party's Central Committee, spelling the end of communist power in Russia. In November, Yeltsin banned the Soviet and Russian Communist Parties altogether. Gorbachev now had no power left to wield, and on 25 December he resigned as president.

Within 24 hours, he and Raisa had to move out of their presidential apartments and their **dacha** and find a new home. All he could do after this was to watch from the sidelines as his country completed the revolution he had begun. At midnight on 31 December 1991, the Soviet Union was officially disbanded, and the title of the **USSR** was wiped from the world map. Russia was now the **Russian Federation** and countries like Ukraine and Estonia became independent.

▼ *Eastern Europe and the break-away republics. East Germany was reunited with West Germany in October 1990. Czechoslovakia later broke into two states – the Czech Republic and Slovakia.*

◄ *Gorbachev, accompanied by his wife Raisa, signs copies of his 1996 memoirs in a London department store.*

Finding a new role

Gorbachev had spent his adult life working, fighting and plotting his way up the political ladder. He found it hard to be an outsider with little influence on events in Russia. But there was still plenty for him to do. Early in 1992 he set up the Gorbachev Foundation in Moscow. Its purpose was to provide a forum (meeting place) for discussing and studying the country's politics, society and economics. He toured both North and South America making speeches and giving interviews. He also travelled the world as the president of Green Cross International, an independent organization dedicated to improving our awareness of the threats to the environment.

Much of Gorbachev's time was taken up with writing his **memoirs**. He was anxious to tell his side of the story and justify his actions as leader of the **Soviet Union**. The book was published in Russia in 1995 and in a number of foreign translations the following year, and was an enormous success, especially abroad. This encouraged him to make one last effort to regain power. He stood as a candidate in the Russian elections for president in 1996, but received less than one per cent of the vote. It was the final rejection.

Gorbachev carried on with his speaking tours and public projects. But fate had another cruel blow to strike. He and Raisa had always done a lot of work for charity, especially in raising money for Russian children suffering from cancer and **leukaemia**. Tragically, Raisa herself died of leukaemia in September 1999.

Gorbachev's legacy

When Mikhail Gorbachev became **general secretary** in 1985, the world was a very different place. The **Cold War** between East and **West** had dominated global events for 40 years. People lived in daily fear of a nuclear conflict which could wipe out their entire civilization. The **Soviet Union** itself was a lumbering, bullying, sickly giant ruled by old men who wanted nothing to change. Gorbachev promised that he could not only reform his country, but bring lasting peace to the world. He succeeded – but not exactly in the way he wanted.

Ending the Cold War

Gorbachev was a surprise to Western leaders. Warm, humorous, sharp and sociable, he was the exact opposite of previous Soviet bosses. He was also willing to make compromises and was sincere in wanting to get rid of **nuclear weapons**.

For a map of the places mentioned, see page 52.

The result was astonishing progress in his **summit** meetings with US presidents Reagan and Bush. Within five years, they had agreed to withdraw huge numbers of troops and weapons from Europe, and the end of the Cold War was in sight.

◀ *The collapse of the Soviet Union created new problems. One of the greatest tragedies took place in the **republic** of Chechnya, which rebelled against continuing Russian control. Russian troops launched a savage and long-running campaign to crush the revolt. This is how the Chechen capital looked in February 2000, after several years of violence. The armoured vehicle is manned by Russian troops.*

► An old woman scavenges for food in Moscow during the severe winter of 1998. The enormous political changes introduced by Gorbachev did nothing to prevent the Russian economic slump, which brought widespread poverty and hardship.

Gorbachev again hurried the peace process along by pulling aside the **Iron Curtain**. He allowed the **Eastern bloc satellite countries** to break free of the Soviet Union and decide their own destinies within Europe. This was probably his finest achievement.

Taking communism apart

His effect on Russia was just as spectacular, but far less successful. 'We had to change everything,' said Gorbachev in his final speech on Russian TV, but he could hardly have known just how devastating that change would be. He believed that his policies of *glasnost* and *perestroika* were going to reform **communism**. He believed that he could rebuild the Soviet Union by lifting state controls, introducing **democratic** elections and encouraging free speech.

He was disastrously wrong. The reforms actually helped to destroy both the Communist Party and the Soviet Union, and Gorbachev himself was swept away in the chaos. On top of this, his policies drove the economy into even deeper trouble. Yet, even though his own plans failed, they gave Russians the chance to change their country forever.

On Gorbachev's part in ending the Cold War:

He may not have done so alone, but what happened would not have happened without him. That cannot be said of anyone else.

(Raymond L. Garthoff, US State Department)

Timeline

1931	March: Mikhail Gorbachev born in Privolnoye, North Caucasus.
1933/34	Famine in Stavropol region.
1941	June: German forces invade **USSR**; Gorbachev's father joins Soviet Army.
1942	August: Germans occupy Stavropol district.
1943	Liberation of the district by Soviet troops.
1950	Becomes candidate member of the **Communist** Party. September: Enters the Law Faculty at Moscow State University.
1952	Becomes full member of the Communist Party.
1953	March: Death of Stalin. September: Gorbachev marries Raisa Titorenko.
1955	June: Graduates from university and returns to Stavropol.
1956	September: Appointed **first secretary** of Stavropol *Komsomol* committee.
1957	January: Birth of daughter Irina.
1958	April: Elected second secretary of local district *Komsomol* committee.
1961	March: Elected first secretary of the same committee.
1962	March: Appointed Party organizer for the region.
1963	January: Appointed head of department for Party organization in Stavropol.
1964	October: Khrushchev dismissed as Party leader; Brezhnev takes power.
1968	August: Soviet troops invade Czechoslovakia.
1970	Gorbachev appointed Party first secretary for Stavropol.
1971	Elected a member of the **Central Committee**.
1972	First trip to the **West** (Belgium and Netherlands).
1978	November: Appointed Secretary for Agriculture; moves with family to Moscow.
1979	November: Elected candidate member of **Politburo**. December: Soviet troops invade Afghanistan.
1980	Gorbachev becomes full member of Politburo.
1982	November: Brezhnev dies and is succeeded by Andropov.
1984	February: Andropov dies and is succeeded by Chernenko.
1985	March: Chernenko dies and is succeeded by Gorbachev.

	November: Gorbachev meets Reagan in their first **summit**, at Geneva.
1986	February: Announces programme of *perestroika* (rebuilding).
	April: Chernobyl **nuclear power plant** disaster.
	July: First troop withdrawals from Afghanistan.
	October: Second summit with Reagan, at Reykjavik.
1987	January: Proposes first political reforms.
	November: Publishes book on *perestroika*.
	Yeltsin resigns from Central Committee.
	December: Gorbachev visits Great Britain and USA.
1988	January: Calls for *glasnost* throughout the press media.
	April: Treaty signed to end Soviet involvement in Afghanistan.
	September: Gorbachev becomes chairman of Supreme Soviet, a powerful arm of government elected by the Congress of Deputies.
	December: Announces major reduction in Soviet armed forces.
1989	March: Free elections for first **Congress of People's Deputies**.
	May: Estonia and Latvia declare independence.
	August: Non-communist government elected in Poland.
	October: Gorbachev travels to Berlin, but refuses to support communist leader.
	November: Fall of the Berlin Wall.
	December: First summit meeting with President Bush, in Malta.
1990	January: Travels to Lithuania, scene of growing unrest.
	February: Free local elections in USSR.
	March: Gorbachev elected president of USSR.
	July/August: More **republics** declare independence.
	October: Gorbachev awarded **Nobel Peace Prize**.
1991	April: Draws up new Union Treaty.
	June: Yeltsin elected Russian president.
	August: Attempted **coup** against Gorbachev fails.
	December: Gorbachev resigns.
1992	January: USSR ceases to exist.
	March: Establishes Gorbachev Foundation in Moscow.
1995	Publication of **memoirs** in Russia.
1996	June: Gorbachev fails to be elected as Russian president.
	October: Memoirs published in English translation.
1999	September: Death of Raisa.

Key people of Gorbachev's time

Andropov, Yuri (1914-84). Became the Soviet **Communist** Party **general secretary** in 1982. People expected a hard line, but he surprised them by calling for world peace and the reduction of **nuclear weapons**.

Brezhnev, Leonid (1906-82). From 1945 he was a close political ally of Khrushchev, whom he succeeded as Soviet Communist Party general secretary in 1964. During his long spell in power he allowed almost no progress, keeping tight control over Eastern Europe and building up Soviet armed forces. He was responsible for the disastrous invasion of Afghanistan in 1979.

Khrushchev, Nikita (1894-1971). As leader of Ukraine in the 1940s he **purged** many opponents of Stalin. After Stalin's death in 1953, he was just as ruthless in getting rid of rivals, becoming chairman of the **Soviet Union** in 1958. He surprised many by his attacks on Stalinism and by his attempt to steer away from rule by terror (for example reducing the power of the **KGB**). He was forced from office in 1964.

Reagan, Ronald (born 1911). Entered politics after a successful career as a film actor. He became president of the USA in 1980 and won a second term in 1984. Though firmly conservative and anti-communist, he was able to form a warm and productive relationship with Gorbachev, which led to great progress in arms reduction.

Stalin, Joseph (1879-1953). Worked closely with Lenin during the **Russian Revolution** of 1917. On Lenin's death he savagely eliminated rivals and by 1927 had became virtual **dictator**, using his **secret police** to suppress all possible opposition. In 1945, he forced or tricked other **Allied leaders** into placing Eastern Europe under his control.

Yeltsin, Boris (born 1931). Gorbachev brought him to the **Kremlin** as head of construction in 1985. Energetic and aggressive, he was forced to resign after his harsh criticism of Gorbachev. Returned as mayor of Moscow and in 1990 became the first **democratically-** elected president of the **Russian Federation**.

Soviet government

The Soviet Union had a parliament (called the Supreme Soviet), elected by the people. However, until 1989, citizens had only one choice – to vote for the candidate selected by the Communist Party. No other party was allowed to put forward candidates. The Party actually controlled the country, and the job of the Supreme Soviet was simply to accept Communist decisions.

The Communist Party of the USSR

The Federal Government

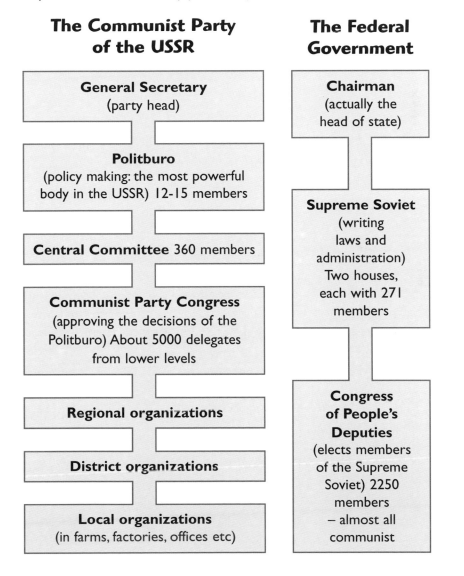

General Secretary
(party head)

Politburo
(policy making: the most powerful body in the USSR) 12-15 members

Central Committee 360 members

Communist Party Congress
(approving the decisions of the Politburo) About 5000 delegates from lower levels

Regional organizations

District organizations

Local organizations
(in farms, factories, offices etc)

Chairman
(actually the head of state)

Supreme Soviet
(writing laws and administration) Two houses, each with 271 members

Congress of People's Deputies
(elects members of the Supreme Soviet) 2250 members
– almost all communist

Where to find out more

Further reading
The Cold War (20th Century Perspectives series), David Taylor, Heinemann Library, 2001

The Fall of the Berlin Wall (Turning Points series), Nigel Kelly, Heinemann Library, 2000

I Hope, Raisa Gorbachev, HarperCollins, 1991

Memoirs, Mikhail Gorbachev, Doubleday, 1996

Websites
Heinemann Explore, an online resource for Key Stage 3 History:
www.heinemannexploresec.com

Website of Green Cross International: Mikhail Gorbachev's home page:
www.gci.ch

Official website of Mikhail Gorbachev:
www.mikhailgorbachev.org

Website of Russia.net, a wide-ranging source of information on Russia:
www.russia.net/~oldrn/history.html

Website of Russia's News Service:
www.nns.ru/e-elects/e-persons/gorbach.html

Sources
Against the Grain: An Autobiography, Boris Yeltsin, Cape, 1990

Cold War, Jeremy Isaacs and Taylor Downing, Bantam, 1998

Down with Big Brother!: The Fall of the Soviet Empire, Michael Dobbs, Knopf, 1997

Gorbachev, Martin McCauley, Longman, 1998

Lenin's Tomb: The Last Days of the Soviet Empire, David Remnick, Random House, 1993

Glossary

Allied leaders leaders of countries that fought together during World War Two on the side of the USA, Britain and France

capitalism economic system which allows free competition and private ownership of the manufacturing and distribution of goods; its main aim is to build up 'capital' (money)

Central Committee main body of the Soviet Communist Party, elected at each Party Congress and containing the most important officials

Cold War uneasy peace (as opposed to a 'hot war') which existed between capitalist and communist countries between the late 1940s and the late 1980s

collective farming system in which labourers were forced to work on state farms; by 1937 this meant all Russian farmland

communism political system, such as that in the Soviet Union, based on state ownership of manufacturing and distribution of goods, centralized planning and government by a single party. A person or party supporting communism is described as communist.

Congress of People's Deputies new and democratically elected parliament for the Soviet Union first convened in 1989; its 2250 deputies were elected for a five year term

coup sudden action taken to gain power or win control

dacha Russian word for a country or holiday house

delegate elected person who represents others

democracy system of government where all are allowed to vote or decide matters freely

dictator ruler who has complete power over government

District Prosecutor lawyer who conducts the prosecution, or case against a person, in criminal proceedings

East Berlin when Germany was divided after World War Two, its capital city Berlin lay in the eastern (communist) half of the country; Berlin was itself divided in two – East (communist) and West (democratic). This division was marked from 1961 by the Berlin Wall.

Eastern bloc countries of Eastern Europe associated with the USSR in the Warsaw Pact

first secretary top official in government or local department

general secretary top Party official in the Soviet Union, and thus the country's leader

glasnost openness in politics and public discussion, plus freedom of information

Iron Curtain imaginary, or sometimes real, barrier that divided the communist East and the capitalist West in Europe

Islam religion based on the teachings of the Prophet Muhammad

KGB 'Committee of State Security', or state police force responsible for controlling and gathering information

Komsomol Young Communist League, open to those aged 14 to 28

Kremlin old fortified centre of Moscow, used as Soviet government headquarters

labour camp prison settlement where inmates are forced to work

leukaemia disease which stops the production of normal blood cells

liberal believing in the freedom of people to act and express themselves as they choose

memoirs in this case an autobiographical account of important events in Soviet Russian history

multi-party system government democratically chosen from several different political parties

Nazis followers of Adolf Hitler in Germany and members of the World War Two German army

Nobel Prize any one of six prizes awarded by the Swedish Nobel Foundation for outstanding achievements in science, literature and world peace

nuclear power plant power station which produces electricity using the energy from the splitting of uranium atoms

nuclear weapons bombs, missiles and other weapons using the destructive power of nuclear energy (the splitting, or fission, of atoms)

one-party system government by a single political party, elected or otherwise

Party Congress most important Communist Party meeting, which took place once in every five-year period to review policies and elect a new Central Committee and Politburo

perestroika 'reforming' or 'rebuilding'; Gorbachev's policy to modernize the Soviet economy

Politburo Political Bureau of the Central Committee, the Party's key decision-making body

political prisoner someone who is imprisoned for his or her political beliefs rather than for a crime

Procurator official who acts for the state as public prosecutor in law cases

propaganda promotion of ideas and information for political purposes

purge to remove all one's opponents or possible enemies by force

radioactive dust particles contaminated with radioactivity (giving out radiation resulting from a nuclear reaction)

Red Banner red flag which was the worldwide symbol of communism

republic country with a constitution and no monarch; in the USSR, a country which is part of a federation but which has some powers to govern itself

resistance fighter someone who fights against the established government of a country

Russian Federation largest of the fifteen Soviet republics (also known simply as Russia)

Russian Revolution uprising of 1917 which overthrew the tsar (monarch) of Russia and gave power to the Bolsheviks, who set up 'soviets' to govern the country and establish a communist state

satellite countries countries controlled by a powerful neighbour, in this case the Soviet Union

secret police police force which works mostly in secret to control dissidents and ensure state security

socialism belief in a social system which is run for the good of the community and in which the means of making and selling goods are owned by everyone. Lenin saw socialism as a midway stage between capitalism and communism.

sovereign state independent country which governs itself

Soviet Union see USSR. The word 'soviet' comes from the name given to elected councils that were set up at the time of the 1917 Russian Revolution.

stagnation condition in which there is no growth or movement

'Star Wars' US project to protect the country from nuclear attack with laser weapons stationed in space; popularly named after the famous film series

state ownership system in which an industry or property belongs to and is controlled by the state government

steppe vast, grass-covered plains stretching from south-east Europe to Siberia

strategic arms weapons so powerful that they dictate the way in which countries organize their defence systems

strike refusing to work as a way of making a protest

summit meeting of the leaders of the most powerful nations

superpower very powerful nation, often using nuclear threat to dominate other countries; during the Cold War, generally applied only to the USA and USSR

trade agreement treaty between countries over the supply of goods or freedom to trade

United Nations Organization international organization of independent countries formed in 1945 to promote international security and cooperation

USSR Union of Soviet Socialist Republics: federation of fifteen national republics in eastern Europe and northern Asia, dominated by Russia and set up in 1922

Warsaw Pact organization of Eastern bloc countries founded in 1955 and pledged to help defend each other in case of attack; created in response to NATO, the North Atlantic Treaty Organization established by the Western powers in 1954

West, Western political, rather than geographical name for the industrialized countries of Western Europe, North America, Australia and New Zealand

Index